Ultimate Cupc

The Ul

CUPCAKE

RECIPE BOOK

50 Delightful Cupcake Recipes for Beginners

By

Les Ilagan

1

Table of Contents

INTRODUCTION

Sugar, spice and everything nice!

This book includes easy cupcake recipes that will surely satisfy your sweet cravings. You'll find here mouth-watering cupcake recipes from vanilla to chocolate and everything in between!

Get inspired with the different cupcake recipes to make your best tasting cupcake ever. Never miss out on your favorite red velvet cupcake recipe and other delightful cupcakes with varying flavors.

You'll find recipes here that will enable you to show off your creativity and improve your baking skills. You can either enjoy making cupcakes for you and your loved ones or even start your very own business, wherein you can customize your cupcakes to suit your client's taste and whatever requirement they may have.

If you are new to baking, no worries! This recipe book is beginner-friendly; it will give you awesome ideas in baking the best tasting cupcakes, making it cheaper than buying from a local store or bakeshop.

Cupcakes are one of the sweetest things that we simply can't resist. These little round cakes are truly versatile because there are many ingredients that you can use to enhance the flavor.

Cupcakes are nice to have for snack, dessert, picnic item, or even serve as party food for any occasion. They make awesome giveaways too or a gift to your loved ones!

This book is a part of many cookbook series that I am writing; I hope you have fun trying all the recipes in this book. So now, let's get it started!

Learn The Basics: Things To Remember In Making The Best Tasting Cupcakes

1. *It is important to use the right ingredients.*

    - Flour power. Different types of flour have different protein contents that affect the texture of your cupcakes. So if the recipe calls for cake flour, use cake flour.

    - Cold eggs? NO! Eggs are used to emulsify the cupcakes properly which causes it to rise. So when baking cupcakes, always use eggs at a room temperature.

    - Good quality ingredients = good quality products. Use the best ingredients that you can have to be able to get those best tasting cupcakes.

2. ***Measure it right.*** Accurate measurement is a must when baking cupcakes!

3. ***Sift dry ingredients together.*** Sifting dry ingredients prevent lumps into the batter. Whisk them after sifting to have an even distribution of all ingredients.

4. ***Cream butter and sugar properly.*** One way of incorporating air into your cupcakes is to cream butter and sugar until light and fluffy.

5. ***Be careful with the batter!*** Do not over mix. Combine dry and wet ingredients just until incorporated. Over mixing results to tough cupcakes!

6. ***Don't forget to preheat the oven properly.*** Make sure that the oven is at right temperature before baking your cupcakes.

7. ***No peeking!*** Opening the oven door during baking causes the cold

air to pass into the cupcakes making them to fall flat.

8. ***Test your cupcakes.*** When time is up, inserting a tooth pick at the center of cupcakes helps to check if it is cooked through. If it comes out clean, then it's done!

9. ***Let it cool.*** Cool cupcakes on a wire rack completely. Frosting on warm cupcakes will melt the frosting and become runny.

10. ***Paper cups or liners are a great help.*** These will catch all the spills and messy frosting.

Homemade Banana Cupcakes

Simple yet tasty cupcake recipe with awesome banana flavor that you'll surely love.

Preparation Time: 15 minutes
Total Time: 45 minutes
Yield: 12 servings

Ingredients
3 ripe bananas, mashed
¾ cup brown sugar
2 large eggs, lightly beaten
½ cup vegetable oil
1 ½ cups all-purpose flour

1 teaspoon baking powder
1 teaspoon baking soda
½ cup buttermilk

Method

1. Preheat the oven to 350F. Line a muffin tin with paper cups.
2. In a bowl, lightly beat bananas and white sugar until smooth. Add eggs one at a time until blended. Stir in vegetable oil.
3. Add the flour, baking powder, baking soda, and buttermilk. Mix until just combined. Pour batter into the muffin cups, about 2/3 full.
4. Bake in the oven for 20 minutes until tested done. Place in wire rack to cool.
5. Serve and enjoy.

Banana Carrot Cupcake with Walnuts

This cupcake recipe has a healthy combination of banana, carrots, and walnuts.

Preparation Time: 15minutes
Total Time: 45 minutes
Yield: 36servings

Ingredients

1 cup sugar
¾ cup olive oil
½ cup buttermilk
2large eggs
2 cups whole meal flour, sifted
1 1/3 teaspoon baking powder, sifted

14

1 1/3 teaspoon baking soda, sifted
1 teaspoon cinnamon, ground
½ teaspoon salt
1 cup carrots, finely grated
1 cup ripe bananas, mashed
½ cup walnuts, chopped

Method

1. Preheat the oven to 375F. Line 3 muffin tins with paper cups.
2. Whisk together sugar, oil, and buttermilk in a large bowl. Add the eggs one at a time until blended well.
3. Add the flour, baking powder, and baking soda; then cinnamon, and salt. Mix until just combined. Fold in the banana, carrots and walnuts.
4. Pour batter to muffin cups, about 2/3 full.
5. Bake in the oven for 20-25 minutes or until tested done. Place in wire racks to cool.
6. Serve and enjoy.

Easy Banana Cashew Cupcakes

A soft and moist cupcake recipe made with bananas and cashews.

Preparation Time: 15 minutes
Total Time: 45 minutes
Yield: 24 servings

Ingredients

1 cup brown sugar
½ cup butter, unsalted
2 large eggs, beaten
2 cups all-purpose flour, sifted
½ teaspoon salt
1 teaspoon baking soda

4medium ripe bananas, mashed
3/4 cup buttermilk
1 teaspoon pure vanilla extract
1 cup cashew nuts, coarsely chopped

Method

1. Preheat the oven to 350F. Line muffin tins with paper cups.
2. In a bowl, cream together sugar and butter. Add the eggs, mixing well before each addition. Sift the flour, salt, and baking soda; add into the sugar mixture. Stir in mashed bananas, buttermilk, and vanilla extract. Mix well. Fold in the chopped cashews.
3. Pour batter into muffin cups, about 2/3 full.
4. Bake in the oven for 20 minutes or until tested done. Place in wire racks to cool.
5. Serve and enjoy!

Yummy Banana Cinnamon Cupcakes

A delicious banana cupcake with a hint of cinnamon.

Preparation Time: 15minutes
Total Time: 45 minutes
Yield: 24servings

Ingredients
2/3 cup brown sugar
1/2 cup vegetable oil
2 large eggs
2/3 cup mashed ripe banana
2/3 cup sour cream
1 teaspoon pure vanilla extract
1 2/3 cups all-purpose flour

1 ½ teaspoon baking powder
1 teaspoon baking soda
½ teaspoon salt
1 teaspoon ground cinnamon

Method

1. Preheat the oven to 350F. Line muffin tins with paper cups.
2. Using a wire whisk, mix together 2/3 cup sugar, oil and eggs in a large bowl. Add in bananas, sour cream, and vanilla. Stir in the dry ingredients just until blended. Pour batter in muffin cups evenly, about 2/3 full.
6. Bake in the oven for 20 minutes or until tested done. Place in wire racks to cool.
3. Serve and enjoy.

Cheesy Citrus Cupcakes

A cheesy cupcake recipe with a mild citrus flavor.

Preparation Time: 15minutes
Total Time: 45 minutes
Yield: 18 servings

Ingredients
1 ¾ cups all-purpose flour, sifted
2 teaspoon baking powder
¼ teaspoon salt
½ cup unsalted butter
¼ cup white sugar
2 large eggs
½ cup condensed milk

¼ cup fresh orange juice
1 teaspoon orange zest
½ cup Velveeta cheese, grated
½ cup cheddar cheese, grated

Method

1. Preheat the oven to 350F. Line muffin tins with paper cups.
2. Combine flour, baking powder and salt in a large bowl.
3. In a separate bowl, beat together the butter, sugar, eggs, condensed milk, orange juice, and zest.
4. Gradually add the flour mixture; mix until just combined.
5. Fold in Velveeta cheese until well blended.
6. Pour batter to muffin cups, about 2/3 full. Sprinkle with cheddar cheese.
7. Bake in the oven for about 20 minutes or until tested done. Cool in wire racks.
8. Serve and enjoy.

Cherry Rhubarb Cupcake

*This cupcake recipe combines the great flavors
of cherry, rhubarb, and almonds.*

Preparation Time: 15 minutes
Total Time: 45 minutes
Yield: 18servings

Ingredients
1 ¾ cups all-purpose flour
1 ½ teaspoon baking powder
½ cup sugar
¾ teaspoon salt
2 egg, lightly beaten
¾ cup milk

½ cup vegetable oil
½ cup rhubarb, chopped
½ cup cherry, pitted and chopped
½ cup almonds, coarsely chopped
6 cherries, pitted and cut in half, for topping

Method

1. Preheat the oven to 350F. Line the muffin tins with paper cups.
2. In a large bowl, mix together the flour, baking powder, sugar, and salt.
3. In a separate bowl, combine egg, milk, and oil. Stir into flour mixture with a wire whisk until moistened and smooth. Fold in rhubarb and cherries.
4. Pour batter to muffin cups, about 2/3 full. Press a cherry on top of each muffin and sprinkle with chopped almonds.
5. Bake in the oven for 20 to 25 minutes or until golden and tested done. Cool in wire racks.
6. Serve and enjoy.

Chocolate Overload Cupcake

*These chocolate cupcakes make a fantastic
party food!*

Preparation Time: 15 minutes
Total Time: 45 minutes
Yield: 18 servings

Ingredients

1 ¾ cups all-purpose flour
1 ½ teaspoons baking powder
½ teaspoon baking soda
½ cup cocoa powder
¾ cup brown sugar
¾ cup semisweet chocolate chips + ¼
cup, for topping

½ cup buttermilk
½ cup water
½ cup vegetable oil
1 large egg
1 teaspoon pure vanilla extract

Method

1. Preheat in the oven to 375 F. Line the muffin tins with baking cups.
2. In a large mixing bowl, combine the flour, baking powder, baking soda, cocoa powder, and sugar.
3. Combine all the liquid ingredients in a separate bowl.
4. Mix together the dry and wet ingredients until just blended. Fold in ¾ cup chocolate chips.
5. Pour batter to muffin cups, about 2/3 full. Top with remaining chocolate chips.
6. Bake in the oven for 15-20 minutes or until cupcakes are tested done. Cool in wire racks.
7. Serve and enjoy.

Moist Deep Chocolate Cupcake

A quick and easy recipe that yields moist and delicious chocolate cupcakes.

Preparation Time: 15minutes
Total Time: 45 minutes
Yield: 18servings

Ingredients
1 ½ cups all-purpose flour
1 cup brown sugar
1 teaspoon baking soda
1 teaspoon salt
½ cup cocoa powder
1 cup water

½ cup vegetable oil
1 teaspoon white vinegar

Method

1. Preheat the oven to 350F. Line the muffin tins with baking cups.
2. In a large bowl, combine flour, baking soda, cocoa, sugar and salt.
3. Combine the water, oil, and vinegar in a separate bowl.
4. Mix together the dry and wet ingredients until just blended and free from lumps.
5. Pour batter into muffin cups, about 2/3 full.
6. Bake in the oven for 20 minutes or until tested done. Place in wire racks to cool.
7. Serve and enjoy.

Chocolate Raspberry Cupcake

A sweet surprise of raspberry-filled chocolate cupcakes with whipped cream and fresh raspberries on top.

Preparation Time: 15minutes
Total Time: 50 hour
Yield: 24 servings

Ingredients

2 cups of all-purpose flour
2/3 cup of cocoa powder, unsweetened
1 teaspoon of baking soda
1 ½ teaspoon of baking powder
½ teaspoon of salt

¾ cup of butter, softened
1 ½ cup of brown sugar
2 large eggs
1 teaspoon pure vanilla extract
1 cup water
½ cup of raspberry preserve or jam
Whipped cream, for topping
Fresh raspberries for garnish

Method

1. Preheat the oven to 350 F. Line muffin tins with paper cups.
2. In a large bowl, combine flour, baking soda, cocoa, baking powder and salt.
3. Beat butter with an electric mixer on high speed for 30 seconds. Add sugar gradually, about ¼ cups at a time on medium speed until combined. Scrape sides of bowl. Beat for at least 2 minutes more until light and fluffy. Add in the eggs, beat well after each addition. Stir in vanilla extract.
4. At low speed, alternately add the flour mixture and water to

the butter mixture until just combined.

5. Spoon batter to muffin cups, about 2/3 full. Smooth out batter using the back of a spoon.

6. Bake in the oven for 20 minutes or when tested done. Place in wire racks to cool.

7. Remove a cone-shape piece of cupcakes using a small paring knife going down only about halfway. Fill each cupcake with 1 teaspoon of raspberry preserve. Top with the removed portion of the cupcake, then top with whipped cream and fresh raspberries.

8. Serve and enjoy.

Double Chocolate Cupcake

Chocolate cupcakes topped with dark chocolate and cream frosting

Preparation Time: 15 minutes
Total Time: 40 minutes
Yield: 18servings

Ingredients

1 ½ cups all-purpose flour
¾ cup sugar
1 teaspoon baking soda
½ cup cocoa powder
½ teaspoon salt
1 cup hot water
½ cup vegetable oil

1 teaspoon vinegar

Dark Chocolate-Cream Frosting:
¾ cup whipped cream
¼ cup icing sugar
¾ cup dark chocolate, melted and cooled

Method

1. Preheat the oven to 375F. Line a muffin tin with paper cups.
2. In a large bowl, combine flour, sugar, baking soda, baking powder, cocoa powder, and salt.
3. Add the hot water, vegetable oil, and vinegar. Mix until smooth.
4. Pour batter to muffin cups, about 2/3 cup full only.
5. Bake in the oven for 18 to 22 minutes or when a toothpick inserted in the center of the cupcakes come out clean. Place in wire racks to cool.
6. **_To make frosting:_** Using an electric mixer on medium speed beat the cream. Gradually add the icing sugar

and continue beating for 1-2 minutes more. Slowly add the melted chocolate. Place in a piping bag then using a star tip, pipe the chocolate frosting onto the cupcakes in circular motion to make a swirl.

7. Serve and enjoy!

Vanilla Cupcake with Butter Cream Frosting

Classic vanilla cupcake topped with delicious butter cream frosting and candy sprinkles.

Preparation Time: 15 minutes
Total Time: 35 minutes
Yield: 18servings

Ingredients

1 2/3 cups all-purpose flour
¾ cup sugar
1 teaspoon baking soda
1 teaspoon baking powder

¾ cup butter, softened
2 egg whites
3 teaspoon vanilla extract
½ cup sour cream
½ cup milk
Candy sprinkles, for topping

Vanilla Butter Cream Frosting:
1 cup butter, softened
1cup powdered sugar
1 teaspoon milk
1 teaspoon pure vanilla extract

Method

1. Preheat the oven to 350F. Line muffin tins with baking cups.
2. In a large bowl, combine flour, baking soda, baking powder, and sugar. On a medium speed, add in butter, egg whites, vanilla, sour cream and milk until smooth. Do not over mix.
3. Pour batter into muffin cups, about 2/3 full.
4. Bake in the oven for 20 to 22 minutes or when a toothpick inserted in the center of the cupcakes comes out clean. Place in wire racks to cool.

5. ***To make Butter Cream frosting:*** In a large mixing bowl, cream butter then gradually add the sugar. Mix for 2 minutes on high speed. Add in milk and vanilla beat further2-3 minutes until smooth and creamy. Transfer frosting in a piping bag.
6. Pipe frosting on top of each cupcake and sprinkle with candy sprinkles.
7. Serve and enjoy!

Basic Lemon Cupcakes

A very soft cupcake recipe bursting with refreshing flavor of lemon.

Preparation Time: 15 minutes
Total Time: 35 minutes
Yield: 18servings

Ingredients

½ cup unsalted butter, softened
¾ cup sugar
2 large eggs
2 teaspoons vanilla extract
1 ½ cup all-purpose flour
2 teaspoon baking powder
½ teaspoon salt

¾ cup milk
Fresh juice and zest of one medium lemon

Method

1. Preheat the oven to 350F. Line muffin pans with paper cups.
2. Beat butter and sugar using a stand mixer fitted with a paddle attachment on a medium-high speed until creamy. Scrape down the both sides of the bowl as needed.
3. Combine the flour, baking powder, and salt in a medium bowl.
4. Slowly add the dry ingredients to the wet ingredients on low speed.
5. Add in milk, lemon zest, and lemon juice. Do not over mix.
6. Pour batter into muffin cups, about 2/3 cup full only.
7. Bake in the oven for 18 to 20 minutes or when tested done. Place in wire racks to cool.
8. Serve and enjoy!

Mocha Cupcakes with Chocolate Chips

A delicious combination of coffee and chocolate that is soft, tender, and moist inside.

Preparation Time: 15 minutes
Total Time: 35 minutes
Yield: 24servings

Ingredients
2 cups of all-purpose flour
1 cup tablespoon sugar
2 teaspoons baking powder
½ teaspoon salt

½ cup butter, warm melted
2 tablespoons cocoa powder
1 tablespoon instant espresso
2 large eggs
3/4 cup milk
1 teaspoon pure vanilla extract
3/4cup semi-sweet chocolate chips

Method

1. Preheat the oven to 375F. Line muffin pans with baking cups.
2. Combine together flour, sugar, baking powder, and salt in a large bowl.
3. Mix together cocoa powder and espresso powder into the warm melted butter in a separate bowl. Stir in milk, eggs, and vanilla extract.
4. Combine the wet and dry ingredients; mix until just blended and free from lumps. Fold in the chocolate chips.
5. Pour batter into the prepared baking cups.
6. Bake in the oven for 18-22 minutes or when tested done. Place in wire racks to cool.

7. Serve and enjoy!

Raspberry Jam Cupcakes

A sweet flavor of raspberry oozing after every bite.

Preparation Time: 10 minutes
Total Time: 35 minutes
Yield: 18 servings

Ingredients

1 ¾ cup all-purpose flour
½ cup sugar
2teaspoons baking powder
2 large eggs
¾ cup milk
½ cup butter, melted

1 teaspoon lemon peel, grated
½ cup raspberry jam

Method

1. Preheat the oven to 350 F. Line 2 muffin tins with baking cups.
2. Combine together the flour, sugar, and baking powder in a large bowl.
3. Lightly beat the eggs in a small bowl. Add the milk, butter, and lemon peel.
4. Mix together the egg mixture and dry ingredients until moistened and no more lumps.
5. Divide half of batter into prepared baking cups. Place a teaspoon of jam into the center of each cup; Spoon remaining batter over jam.
6. Bake in the oven for 18-22 minutes or until tested done. Place in wire racks to cool.
7. Top each cupcake with remaining jam.
8. Serve and enjoy!

Easy Red Velvet Cupcakes with Homemade Cream Cheese Frosting

Enjoy these red velvet cupcakes topped with lovely vanilla cream cheese frosting!

Preparation Time: 15minutes
Total Time: 40 minutes
Yield: 24 servings

Ingredients
2 cups of all-purpose flour
1cup of brown sugar
¼ cup of cocoa powder
1 teaspoon of baking powder

1 teaspoon of baking soda
½ teaspoon of salt
1 cup of buttermilk
2/3 cup of vegetable oil
2 large eggs
2 teaspoons of red food coloring
1 teaspoon of white vinegar
1 teaspoon of pure vanilla extract

Vanilla Cream Cheese Frosting:
1 cup of cream cheese
¾ cup of whipped cream
1 teaspoon of pure vanilla extract
¾ cup of powdered sugar

Method

1. Preheat the oven to 350F. Line the muffin tins with paper cups.
2. Combine together the flour, brown sugar, cocoa powder, baking soda, and salt in a large bowl.
3. In another bowl, mix together the buttermilk, vegetable oil, eggs, red food coloring, white vinegar, and vanilla extract using a handheld electric mixer.

4. Combine dry ingredients into the buttermilk mixture until well blended.

5. Pour batter into muffin cups, about 2/3 full.

6. Bake for 20-22 minutes or until tested done. Cool completely on wire racks.

7. ***To make the Vanilla Cream Cheese frosting***: Beat together the cream cheese, cream, and vanilla extract in a large mixing bowl until smooth. On a low speed, gradually add in the powdered sugar until combined. Shift the speed to medium high and mix further 2-3 minutes.

8. Spread frosting on top of each cupcake. You may sprinkle it with crumbled red velvet cupcake.

9. Serve and enjoy!

Pumpkin Spice Cupcakes

A satisfying pumpkin cupcake recipe with cinnamon-spiced cream cheese frosting.

Preparation Time: 15 minutes
Total Time: 45 minutes
Yield: 24 servings

Ingredients

2 ¼ cups of all-purpose flour
½ teaspoon of cinnamon, ground
½ teaspoon of nutmeg
½ teaspoon of ginger, grated
½ teaspoon of cloves, ground
½ teaspoon of salt
2 teaspoons of baking powder

1 teaspoon of baking soda
2/3 cup of butter, softened
1 cup of brown sugar
2 large eggs
¾ cup of milk
1 cup of pumpkin puree
Brown sugar, for sprinkling
Ground cinnamon, for sprinkling

Cinnamon-Spiced Cream Cheese Frosting:
1 cup cream cheese, softened
¼ cup of butter, softened
1 teaspoon of pure vanilla extract
1 teaspoon cinnamon, ground
1 cup of icing sugar, sifted

Method
1. Preheat the oven to 375F. Line 2 muffin pans with baking cups.
2. In a medium mixing bowl, sift together the flour, 1 teaspoon cinnamon, nutmeg, ginger, clove, salt, baking powder, and baking soda.
3. In a separate bowl, beat ½ cup butter and brown sugar using an electric mixer until creamy and fluffy.

4. Add in the eggs on at a time allowing each egg to blend well into the butter mixture. Stir in the milk and pumpkin puree after the last egg. Stir in the flour mixture until just blended.

5. Pour batter into the muffin cups, about 2/3 cup full only.

6. Bake in the oven for 20-22 minutes or until golden brown and tested done. Cool completely on wire racks.

7. ***To make the Cinnamon-Spiced Cream Cheese frosting:*** beat together the cream cheese, ¼ butter, vanilla, and cinnamon using an electric mixer until smooth; slowly add in the icing sugar and beat until fluffy.

8. Spread frosting on top of each cupcake. Sprinkle with some brown sugar and cinnamon.

9. Serve and enjoy!

Vanilla Cupcakes with Easy Strawberry Cream Cheese Frosting

These delicious vanilla cupcakes with an elegant strawberry cream cheese frosting is a sure hit at parties!

Preparation Time: 15 minutes
Total Time: 45 minutes
Yield: 18servings

Ingredients

1 2/3 cups all-purpose flour
¾ cup white sugar
1 teaspoon baking soda

1 teaspoon baking powder
¾ cup butter, softened
3 egg whites
1 teaspoon vanilla extract
½ cup sour cream
½ cup milk
Pink pearl candies, for topping

Strawberry Cream Cheese Frosting:
1cup cream cheese, softened
¼ cup butter, softened
½ cup icing sugar, sifted
½ cup strawberry jam

Method

1. Preheat the oven to 350F. Line 2 muffin pans with paper cups.
2. In a large bowl, combine the flour, white sugar, baking soda, and baking powder.
3. On a medium speed, add in butter, egg whites, vanilla, sour cream, and milk until smooth. Do not over mix.
4. Pour batter into the muffin cups, about 2/3 cup full only.
5. Bake in the oven for 18 to 20 minutes or until tested done. Place in wire racks to cool.

6. ***To make Strawberry Cream Cheese frosting:*** Using an electric mixer, combine together cream cheese and butter until smooth and fluffy. On low speed, gradually add icing sugar and strawberry jam. Shift speed to medium until mixture becomes fluffy. You may more sugar to achieve desired consistency.

7. Spread frosting on top of each cupcake. Sprinkle with pink pearl candies.

8. Serve and Enjoy!

Lemon Cupcakes with Lemon Butter Cream Frosting

This cupcake recipe is bursting with the flavor of lemon combined with butter cream frosting.

Preparation Time: 15minutes
Total Time: 45 minutes
Yield: 12 servings

Ingredients
¾ cup all-purpose flour
¾ cup cake flour
1 teaspoon baking powder
1/8 teaspoon baking soda
¼ teaspoon salt

¾ cup white sugar
1 tablespoon lemon zest, finely grated
½ cup butter, softened
1 large egg
2 large egg whites
½ cup milk
2 tablespoons lemon juice

Lemon Butter Cream Frosting:
1 cup butter, softened
1 ½ teaspoon fresh lemon zest
1 ½ cup powdered sugar
1 tablespoon lemon juice
1 tablespoon heavy cream
½ teaspoon pure vanilla extract
¼ teaspoon lemon extract

Method

1. Preheat the oven to 350F. Line one muffin tin with paper cups.
2. In a mixing bowl, sift together all-purpose flour and cake flour. Add in baking powder, baking soda and salt. Set aside.
3. Whip together butter with sugar and lemon zest in the bowl of an electric stand mixer until pale and fluffy.

4. Add the eggs one at a time then gradually add the milk and lemon juice.

5. Add the flour mixture into the wet mixture and continue mixing until just combined. Scrape down sides and bottom of the bowl, if needed.

6. Pour batter to muffin cups, about 2/3 cup full only.

7. Bake in the oven for 18 to 20 minutes or until tested done. Place in wire rack to cool.

8. ***To make Lemon Butter Cream frosting:*** Whip butter with lemon zest in the bowl of the electric stand mixer on medium-high speed until very pale and fluffy. Slowly add in powdered sugar, then lemon juice, cream, and vanilla extract. Beatfrosting mixture until very fluffy. Transfer in a piping bag with star tip.

9. Pipe the frosting in a circular motion to make a swirl on top of each lemon cupcake.

Sprinkle with finely grated lemon zest, if desired.

10. Serve and enjoy!

Vanilla Cupcake with Rich Chocolate Frosting

This fluffy vanilla cupcake recipe with rich chocolate frosting is perfect for kiddie birthday parties!

Preparation Time: 15 minutes
Total Time: 45 minutes
Yield: 12 servings

Ingredients

1 2/3 cups all-purpose flour
1 cup sugar
½ teaspoon baking soda
1 teaspoon baking powder

¾ cup butter, softened
2 large eggs
1 teaspoon pure vanilla extract
½ cup milk
½ cup sour cream
Rainbow candy sprinkles

Rich Chocolate Frosting:
1 cup butter, softened
1 ½ cups icing sugar
¾ cup unsweetened cocoa powder
1 teaspoons pure vanilla extract
3 tablespoons heavy cream

Method

1. Preheat oven to 350F. Line one muffin tin with paper cups.
2. In a large bowl, combine the flour, sugar, baking soda, and baking powder. On a medium speed, add in butter, eggs, vanilla extract, milk, and sour cream until smooth. Do not over mix.
3. Pour batter to muffin cups, about 2/3 cup full only.
4. Bake in the oven for 18 to 20 minutes or until tested done. Place in wire rack to cool.

5. ***To make Rich Chocolate frosting:*** Cream the butter on high speed using a handheld or electric stand mixer. Gradually add the icing sugar, cocoa powder on a low speed. Beat until sugar and cocoa are absorbed into the butter. Add vanilla and cream then shift to medium-high and beat further 1 minute. Transfer chocolate frosting in a piping bag with start tip.

6. Pipe frosting in a circular motion to make a swirl on top of each vanilla cupcake. Sprinkle with rainbow candy sprinkles.

7. Serve and enjoy!

Basic Chocolate Mint Cupcakes

Feel the coolness of peppermint in every bite of this chocolate cupcake!

Preparation Time: 15 minutes
Total Time: 45 minutes
Yield: 18 servings

Ingredients
1 cup semi-sweet chocolate, melted
2/3 cup butter, melted
1 ½ cup sugar
2large eggs
1 teaspoon mint extract

2 cups all-purpose flour, sifted
1 teaspoon baking powder
1 teaspoon baking soda
1 cup water

Method

1. Preheat the oven to 350F. Line 2 muffin pans with baking cups.
2. Using an electric mixer, combine melted chocolate, butter, sugar, and vanilla; beat until well blended.
3. Add in the eggs one at a time until blended well.
4. On low speed, gradually add the flour, baking powder, baking soda, and water. Mix until smooth.
5. Pour batter into muffin cups, about 2/3 cup full only.
6. Bake in the oven for 20 to 25 minutes or until tested done. Place in wire racks to cool.
7. Serve and enjoy!

Valentine Cupcakes with Vanilla Cream Cheese Frosting

Soft and fluffy strawberry cupcakes filled with vanilla cream cheese frosting.

Preparation Time: 15minutes
Total Time: 45 minutes
Yield: 12 servings

Ingredients

1 2/3 cups all-purpose flour
¾ teaspoon baking powder
¾ teaspoon baking soda

¼ teaspoon salt
½ cup melted butter, unsalted
1 cup white sugar
½ cup milk
½ cup strawberry puree
1 large egg
2 egg whites
1 teaspoon pure vanilla extract
Heart-shaped candy sprinkles, for topping

Simple Vanilla Cream Cheese Frosting:
1 ½ cups cream cheese
1cup icing sugar
1 teaspoon pure vanilla extract

Method

1. Preheat the oven to 350F. Line a muffin tin with baking cups.
2. Combine flour, baking powder, baking soda, and salt in a medium mixing bowl. Set aside.
3. In a separate bowl, cream butter until lightly fluffy using an electric mixture at a medium high speed. Add the sugar bit by bit and mix until blended well. Add the eggs one at a time at a low speed. Stir in vanilla extract.

4. Combine milk and strawberry puree. Pour into the butter mixture.
5. Slowly add the dry ingredients. Mix until smooth. Scrape down the sides of bowl, if needed.
6. Pour batter to muffin cups, about 2/3 cup full only.
7. Bake in the oven for 20 to 22 minutes or until tested done. Place in a wire rack to cool.
8. ***To make Simple Vanilla Cream Cheese frosting:*** Using an electric mixer, mix together the cream cheese, icing sugar, and vanilla extract on medium speed for 3-4 minutes. Transfer in a piping bag with star tip.
9. Pipe frosting in circular motion to make a swirl on top of each cupcake. Sprinkle with heart-shaped candy sprinkles.
10. Serve and enjoy!

Chocolate Cupcakes with Vanilla Butter Cream Frosting

A rich and creamy combination of chocolate cupcakes with vanilla butter cream frosting.

Preparation Time: 15minutes
Total Time: 40 minutes
Yield: 24servings

Ingredients

2 cups of cake flour, sifted
¾ teaspoon baking soda
¾ teaspoon baking powder
½ teaspoon salt

1cup sugar
¾ cup unsalted butter, softened
6 ounces unsweetened chocolate, melted
1 teaspoon pure vanilla extract
2 large eggs
1 cup water

Vanilla Butter Cream Frosting:
1 cup unsalted butter, softened
1cup icing sugar
1/8 teaspoon salt
1 teaspoon milk
1 teaspoon pure vanilla extract

Method
1. Preheat in the oven to 325F. Line 2 muffin tins with baking cups.
2. Combine the cake flour, baking powder, baking soda and salt in a medium bowl.
3. In a separate bowl, cream together butter and sugar until light in color and fluffy using an electric mixer fitted with paddle attachment for 3 to 5 minutes.
4. On a medium speed, add in chocolate and vanilla extract; beat until well combined. Add in

eggs one at a time, mixing well every after each addition.

5. Add flour mixture in parts on low speed alternating with water (starting and ending with flour). Continue to mix until just incorporated.

6. Pour batter into muffin cups, about 2/3 cup full only.

7. Bake in the oven for 20 minutes or until tested done. Place in wire racks to cool.

8. ***To make Vanilla Butter Cream frosting:*** Using an electric mixer beat unsalted butter, icing sugar, and salt in a medium bowl until blended well. Add in milk and vanilla; beat until smooth and creamy for 3 to 5 minutes on medium-high speed. Transfer in a piping bag with star tip.

9. Pipe frosting in circular motion to make a swirl on top of each cupcake.

10. Serve and enjoy!

Oreo Cupcakes with Cookies and Cream Frosting

A delightful chocolate cupcake topped with Oreo butter cream frosting.

Preparation Time: 15minutes
Total Time: 45 minutes
Yield: 24 servings

Ingredients

¾ cup unsalted butter, at room temperature
¾ cup white sugar
2 cups cake flour, sifted
½ cup pure cocoa powder, sifted
1 teaspoon baking soda

½ teaspoon salt
2 large eggs
¾ cup water
¼ cup buttermilk
1 teaspoon pure vanilla extract
10 Oreo cookies, coarsely chopped

Cookies and Cream Frosting:
1 cup whipped cream
1 ½ cups powdered sugar
½ teaspoon vanilla extract
8Oreo cookies, finely crushed
10 Oreo cookies cut into half for garnish

Method

1. Preheat the oven to 375F. Line 2 muffin tins with baking cups.
2. In the bowl of an electric mixer, cream the butter and sugar using paddle attachment on medium-high speed. Add the eggs one at a time, beating thoroughly after each addition.
3. Add the water, buttermilk, and vanilla. Mix well.
4. Gradually add flour, cocoa powder, baking powder, and salt. Beat on low speed until

just combined. Fold in chopped Oreos.

5. Pour batter into muffin cups, about 2/3 cup full only.

6. Bake for 15 to 20 minutes or until tested done. Place in wire racks to cool.

7. ***To make Oreo Butter Cream frosting:*** beat the cream in the bowl of an electric mixer on medium-high speed until creamy and fluffy for about 3 minutes. Reduce speed to low then add powdered sugar gradually until thoroughly mixed. Shift to high and beat for 2-3 minutes. Add vanilla extract and Oreo crumbs. Mix well. Transfer in a piping bag with star tip.

8. Pipe frosting in circular motion to make a swirl on top of each cupcake.

9. Top cupcakes with half of an Oreo cookie.

10. Serve and enjoy!

Rainbow Cupcake with Easy Butter Cream Frosting

A colorful cupcake with butter cream frosting to brighten up your day

Preparation Time: 15 minutes
Total Time: 40 minutes
Yield: 24 servings

Ingredients

1 (18 ounces) box yellow cake mix
2large eggs
½ cup vegetable oil
½ cup water
8 ounces sour cream
1 small vanilla instant pudding

Food coloring (red, blue, yellow, green, and purple)

Easy Butter Cream Frosting:
1 cup unsalted butter, softened
1 ½ cups icing sugar
1 tablespoon heavy cream
1 teaspoon pure vanilla extract
1/8 teaspoon salt

Method
1. Preheat the oven to 350F. Line 2 muffin tins with baking cups.
2. Mix together the cake mix, eggs, oil, water, sour cream and pudding in the bowl of an electric mixer with paddle attachment on a medium speed until well combined.
3. Divide the batter evenly into 5 small bowls. Drop a few drops of each food color onto each cake batter until desired color is reached. Stir well.
4. Into the lined baking cups, spoon each color until 2/3 of the cup is filled.

5. Bake in the oven for 20 minutes or until tested done. Place in wire racks to cool.

6. ***To make Easy Butter Cream frosting:*** In a medium mixing bowl, combine butter, icing sugar, and salt until well blended. Add in heavy cream and vanilla beat for 3 to 5 minutes or until smooth and creamy. Transfer in a piping bag then pipe in circular motion to make a swirl on top of each cupcake.

7. Serve and enjoy.

Homemade Ban Apple Cupcake

An easy to make cupcake recipe banana, apple, and cinnamon.

Preparation Time: 15minutes
Total Time: 45 minutes
Yield: 24 servings

Ingredients

2 cups whole wheat flour
1 teaspoon baking soda
1 teaspoon salt
1 teaspoon ground cinnamon

1/3 cup applesauce
1/3 cup vegetable oil
1 1/4 cups brown sugar
2 large eggs
1 teaspoon vanilla extract
1/3 cup buttermilk
1 cup mashed ripe bananas
2 medium apples, peeled, cored, and finely chopped
Whipped vanilla frosting, ready to use
Ground cinnamon, for sprinkling
Ground nutmeg, for sprinkling

Method

1. Preheat the oven to 375 F. Line 2 muffin tins with paper cups.
2. Sift the flour, baking soda, salt, and cinnamon. Set aside.
3. In a large bowl, mix together the apple sauce, vegetable oil, and brown sugar using an electric mixer on medium speed until blended well.
4. Beat in the eggs one at a time, and then add in the vanilla and buttermilk.
5. Slowly add in the flour mixture, mixing just until combined.

6. Fold in the mashed bananas and chopped apples. Fill each muffin cup, about2/3 full.
7. Bake in the oven for 20 to 25 minutes, or until tested done. Cool in wire racks.
8. Top with whipped vanilla frosting and sprinkle with ground cinnamon and nutmeg.
9. Serve and enjoy.

Homemade Peppermint Cupcakes

A delicious and very festive dessert or snack recipe perfect for the holidays!

Preparation Time: 15minutes
Total Time: 45 minutes
Yield: 12 pieces

Ingredients
6 candy canes, cut into small pieces
1 2/3 cups whole wheat flour
½ teaspoon baking soda
1 teaspoon baking powder
¾ cup butter, softened

¾ cup sugar
2 large eggs
½ cup milk
½ cup sour cream
1 teaspoon peppermint extract
Whipped vanilla frosting, ready to use

Method

1. Preheat the oven to 350F. Line the muffin tin with paper cups.
2. In a food processor, finely chop the candy canes. Set aside.
3. Sift the flour, baking soda, and baking powder. Set aside.
4. In a large bowl, cream the butter and sugar until fluffy using an electric mixer on medium-high speed. Add the eggs one at a time. Add the vanilla, milk, sour cream, and peppermint extract.
5. On low speed, gradually add the flour mixture until blended. Fold in half of the chopped candy canes.
6. Pour batter into baking cups, about 2/3 cup filled.

7. Bake in the oven for 20-22 minutes or until tested done. Place in wire racks to cool.
8. Stir in remaining candy canes into the whipped vanilla frosting while cupcakes are cooling.
9. Place frosting in a piping bag with star tip. Pipe onto each cupcake. Garnish with more candy canes, if desired.
10. Serve and enjoy.

Pink Lemonade Cupcake

A luscious pink cupcake recipe, great for parties!

Preparation Time: 15minutes
Total Time: 35 minutes
Yield: 12 pieces

Ingredients

1 ½ cups all-purpose flour
1½ teaspoons baking powder
½ teaspoon baking soda
½ cup sugar
½ cup canola oil
2 large eggs
¼ cup pink lemonade concentrate

¾ cup milk

Pink Lemonade Frosting:
1 ½ cup icing sugar
¾ cup unsalted butter
1 pinch salt
¼ cup whipping cream
2 teaspoons pink lemonade concentrate
1 teaspoon lemon extract
2-3 drops red food coloring

Method

1. Preheat the oven to 350F. Line the muffin tin with baking cups.
2. Sift the flour, baking powder, and baking soda in a medium bowl. Set aside.
3. Using an electric mixer, beat together the sugar, oil, eggs and lemonade concentrate in a large bowl until smooth.
4. Add in flour mixture and milk alternately, making three additions of flour mixture and two of milk, until smooth.
5. Pour batter into baking cups, about 2/3 full.

6. Bake in the oven for 20 to 25 minutes or until tested done. Place in wire racks to cool.

7. ***To make Pink Lemonade Frosting:*** Beat the sugar, butter, salt using an electric mixer on a medium speed until creamy. Increase speed to high and beat until fluffy. Add the whipped cream, lemon concentrate, lemon extract, and 2-3 drops of red food color; beat further 2 minutes.

8. Serve and enjoy.

Tropical Citrus Spice Cupcakes

A taste of orange, spice and a coconut surprise inside topped with creamy orange flavored frosting

Preparation Time: 20minutes
Total Time: 50 minutes
Yield: 24servings

Ingredients

2 ½ cups cake flour
1 teaspoon baking powder
1 teaspoon baking soda

¼ teaspoon salt
1 teaspoon cinnamon, ground
½ teaspoon ginger, ground
¼ teaspoon nutmeg, ground
¼ teaspoon cloves, ground
½ cup butter, unsalted
1 ¼ cup brown sugar
2 large eggs
1 tablespoon orange liqueur
¼ cup freshly squeezed orange
½ cup coconut milk
½ cup buttermilk
½ cup coconut flakes
Orange zest, finely grated, for topping

Orange Vanilla Frosting:
2 cups whipped vanilla frosting, ready to use
2 ounces cream cheese
2 tablespoons orange juice
1tablespoonorange liqueur

Method
1. Preheat the oven to 350F. Line the muffin tins with paper cups.
2. Sift the flour, baking powder, baking soda, salt, cinnamon, ginger, nutmeg, and coves in a

medium bowl. Combine the mixture lightly until everything is mixed throughout.

3. Using an electric mixer, cream butter until soft and fluffy on medium-high speed. Add in sugar and eggs and beat until fluffy about 3-5 minutes. Add in orange liqueur until incorporated.

4. Add ¼ cup orange juice and 1/3 of flour mixture and beat until incorporated scraping the mixture down into the bowl as needed.

5. Add in coconut milk and ½ of the remaining flour mixture and beat until combined. Add the buttermilk and the remaining of the flour mixture; beat again until incorporated. Fold in coconut flakes onto the mixture until blended.

6. Pour batter into baking cups, about 2/3 full.

7. Bake in the oven for 20 minutes or until tested done. Place in wire racks to cool.

8. ***To make Orange Vanilla frosting:*** In a medium bowl, beat the whipped vanilla frosting, cream cheese, orange juice, orange liqueur until smooth, about 2-3 minutes.
9. Top cupcakes with frosting and sprinkle with orange zest.
10. Serve and enjoy!

Moist Banana Walnut Cupcake

Moist and soft banana cupcake recipe with walnuts.

Preparation Time: 15minutes
Total Time: 45 minutes
Yield: 12 servings

Ingredients

½ cup butter, softened
¾ cup brown sugar
1 teaspoon vanilla extract
2 large eggs
1 cup all-purpose flour

1 teaspoon baking powder
½ teaspoon baking soda
½ teaspoon ground nutmeg
¼ teaspoon salt
½ cup sour cream
½ cup ripe banana, mashed
½ cup walnuts, chopped

Method

1. Preheat the oven to 350F. Line the muffin tin with paper cups.
2. Cream the butter and sugar, and vanilla in a large bowl with an electric mixer set to medium-high speed for 2-3 minutes. Add eggs one at a time. Beat well after each addition.
3. Sift together the flour, baking soda, nutmeg and salt. Gradually add onto cream mixture alternately with sour cream. Mix well after each addition. Fold in the mashed banana and half of the walnuts.
4. Pour batter into baking cups, about 2/3 full. Sprinkle with remaining walnuts.

5. Bake in the oven for 18 to 22 minutes or until tested done. Place in wire racks to cool.
6. Serve and enjoy.

Caramel Apple Cupcake

You simply can't go wrong with this awesome cupcake recipe with apple and caramel sauce topping!

Preparation Time: 15minutes
Total Time: 45 minutes
Yield: 24 servings

Ingredients
2 ¼ cups all-purpose flour
2 teaspoons baking powder
1 teaspoon baking soda
1 teaspoon apple pie spice
1/4 teaspoon salt
½ cup applesauce

¼ cup vegetable oil
¾ cup brown sugar
2 large eggs
½ cup half-and-half cream
Whipped vanilla frosting, for topping

Apple Caramel Sauce:
½ cup condensed milk
¼ cup brown sugar
2 tablespoon butter
3 medium apples, peeled, cored and diced
½ teaspoon cinnamon, ground

Method

1. Preheat the oven to 350F. Line the muffin tins with paper cups.
2. In a medium bowl, sift the flour, baking powder, baking soda, apple pie spice, and salt.
3. In a large bowl, mix together applesauce, vegetable oil, and brown sugar set to a medium speed. Add the eggs one at a time then the half and half cream. Continue beating for 2 minutes, scraping bowl often. On low speed, gradually add

the flour-spice mixture and stir until just combined.

4. Pour batter into baking cups, about 2/3 full.

5. Bake in the oven for 18 to 22 minutes or until tested done. Place in wire racks to cool.

6. ***To make Apple Caramel Sauce***: Combine condensed milk, brown sugar and butter in a saucepan. Cook for 5 minutes over medium heat. Reduce heat to medium-low then add the apples and cinnamon; cook further 5-7 minutes.

7. Top each cupcake with whipped vanilla frosting and Apple Caramel Sauce.

8. Serve and enjoy.

Homemade Fresh Blueberry Cupcake

This cupcake recipe is bursting with the fresh flavor of blueberries in each and every bite!

Preparation Time: 15 minutes
Total Time: 45 minutes
Yield: 24servings

Ingredients
¾ cup unsalted butter
1 ¼ cups brown sugar
1 teaspoon pure vanilla extract
2 large eggs
2 ¼ cups all-purpose flour

93

1 ½ teaspoon baking powder
1 teaspoon baking soda
½ teaspoon salt
¾ cup buttermilk
1½ cups blueberries

Method

1. Preheat the oven to 350F. Line 2 muffin tins with paper cups.
2. In a medium bowl, with an electric mixer set to medium-high speed, cream the unsalted butter, brown sugar, and vanilla extract. Add the eggs one at a time.
3. Sift dry ingredients in a large bowl. Slowly combine dry mixture into the butter mixture. Adding some of the milk alternating with flour until combined. Do not over mix. Fold in blueberries.
4. Pour batter into baking cups, about 2/3 full.
5. Bake in the oven for 25 minutes or until tested done. Place in wire racks to cool.
6. Serve and enjoy!

Almond Lime Cupcake

A wonderful cupcake recipe made with almond and lime.

Preparation Time: 15minutes
Total Time: 45 minutes
Yield: 12 servings

Ingredients

¼ cup lime juice, freshly squeezed
1 teaspoon lime zest, freshly grated
1 cup almond milk
¼ cup vegetable oil
½ teaspoon pure vanilla extract
¾ cup sugar
1 cup all-purpose flour, sifted

1/3 cup almond flour, sifted
1 teaspoon baking powder
½ teaspoon baking soda
¼ teaspoon salt
Ready to use whipped vanilla frosting
Lime wedges, for garnish
Finely grated lime zest, for sprinkling

Method

1. Preheat the oven to 350F. Line the muffin tin with paper cups.
2. In a medium bowl, with an electric mixer set to medium speed, mix together lime juice, zest, milk, oil, vanilla and sugar.
3. Combine flour, baking soda, baking powder, and salt in a separate medium bowl then slowly add onto the wet mixture and continue mixing until smooth. Do not over mix.
4. Pour batter into baking cups, about2/3 cups full.
5. Bake for 20 to 25 minutes or until tested done. Place in wire racks to cool.
6. Top each cupcake with whipped vanilla frosting.

Sprinkle with lime zest and garnish with lime wedge.

7. Serve and enjoy.

Maple Lemon Cupcake

A sweet and tangy cupcake recipe that is perfect for picnics or tea time!

Preparation Time: 15minutes
Total Time: 45minutes
Yield: 24servings

Ingredients
1 cup all-purpose flour
1 ¼ cup cake flour
1 ½ teaspoon baking powder
½ teaspoon bicarbonate soda
½ teaspoon salt
¾ cup unsalted butter
½ cup brown sugar

2 large eggs
½ cup half-and-half
½ cup milk
¼ cup maple syrup
¼ cup lemon juice

Creamy Maple Lemon Frosting:
1 (8 ounces) package cream cheese
2 tablespoons unsalted butter
¾ cup powdered sugar
¼ cup maple syrup
1 ½ teaspoon lemon zest, finely grated
2 drops yellow food coloring

Method

1. Preheat the oven to 350 F. Line the muffin tins with paper cups.
2. Sift all-purpose flour, cake flour, baking powder, baking soda, and salt in a medium bowl.
3. Cream the butter and brown sugar in the bowl of a mixer set to medium speed. Add in vanilla and eggs (one at a time). Mixture should be fluffy and light.

4. Add the half and half cream, milk, maple, and lemon juice until combined well.
5. Add the flour mixture gradually mix until just blended.
6. Pour batter into baking cups, about 2/3 full.
7. Bake in the oven for 20-22 minutes or until tested done. Place in wire racks to cool.
8. ***To make the Creamy Maple Lemon frosting:*** Using an electric mixer set to medium speed, beat the cream cheese and butter until fluffy and smooth. Bit by bit add the powdered sugar then the maple syrup, lemon zest, and food coloring. Beat further 3-5 minutes. Transfer in a piping bag.
9. Pipe frosting onto each cupcake in circular motion to make a swirl.
10. Serve and enjoy.

Cookies and Cream Cheesecake Cups

A perfect treat for all cookies and cream and cheesecake lovers!

Preparation Time: 15minutes
Total Time: 1 hour
Yield: 30 servings

Ingredients

30 Oreo cookies, whole
12Oreo cookies, chopped
2 (8 ounces) cream cheese
1 cup sour cream
1 cup condensed milk

1 teaspoon pure vanilla extract
4 large eggs

Method

1. Preheat the oven to 275F. Line the muffin tins with baking cups.
2. Beat cream cheese using an electric mixer set to medium-high speed until smooth scraped down sides of the bowl, if needed. Add the sour cream, condensed milk, and vanilla extract; continue beating until combined.
3. Add eggs one at a time then fold in chopped Oreos.
4. For each muffin cup, place 1 piece Oreo then pour the batter over, about 3/4 cupful.
5. Bake in the oven for about 35-45 minutes or until tested done. Place in wire racks to cool.
6. Refrigerate until ready to serve.
7. Enjoy.

Marshmallow Popcorn Cupcake

A creative way to decorate your cupcakes using marshmallows!

Preparation Time: 20minutes
Total Time: 20 minutes
Yield: 12 servings

Ingredients

12freshly baked vanilla cupcakes
Ready to use white icing or whipped
vanilla frosting, for topping
Mini yellow marshmallows, for topping

Method

1. Frost each cupcake with white icing.
2. Cut one mini marshmallow in half and squish the two pieces back together into whole mini marshmallow, pinching firmly. Press some of the finished marshmallow popcorn onto each of the frosted cupcake.
3. Serve and enjoy!

Yummy Nutella Cupcake

This Nutella flavored cupcake recipe makes a great grab and go food for breakfast or snack.

Preparation Time: 15 minutes
Total Time: 45 minutes
Yield: 12 servings

Ingredients
½ cup butter, softened
½ cup white sugar
¼ cup Nutella
2 large eggs
1 ¾ cups sifted all-purpose flour
¼ teaspoon salt

1 ¼ teaspoons baking powder
½ teaspoon baking soda
2/3 cup buttermilk
Nutella, for topping
Chopped hazelnuts, for topping

Method

1. Preheat the oven to 350F. Line the muffin tin with paper cups.
2. In a large bowl, with an electric mixer set to medium speed, cream together the butter, white sugar, and ¼ cup Nutella until blended well and fluffy.
3. Add eggs one at a time until well blended. Gradually add in the flour alternately with buttermilk; then add the salt, baking powder, and baking soda; mix until combined well.
4. Pour batter into baking cups, about 3/4full.
5. Bake in the oven for 20 minutes or until tested done. Place in wire racks to cool.
6. Spread 2 teaspoons of Nutella evenly on each cupcake.

Sprinkle with chopped hazelnuts.

7. Serve and enjoy.

Butterfinger Cupcake Recipe

A quick and easy chocolate cupcake recipe with the addition of an all-time favorite candy bar – Butterfinger.

Preparation Time: 15minutes
Total Time: 45 minutes
Yield: 18servings

Ingredients

1 ¾ cups all-purpose flour
1 ½ teaspoons baking powder
½ teaspoon baking soda
2 tablespoons cocoa powder
¾ cup brown sugar

½ cup water
¼ cup buttermilk
½ cup vegetable oil
1 large egg
1 teaspoon pure vanilla extract
2 pieces Nestle Butterfinger, chopped
Ready to use whipped vanilla frosting

Method

1. Preheat the oven to 350F. Line the muffin tins with paper cups.
2. In a large mixing bowl, combine the all-purpose flour, baking powder, baking soda, cocoa powder, and brown sugar.
3. Combine all the liquid ingredients in a separate bowl.
4. Mix together the dry and wet ingredients until just blended. Fold in half of the chopped Butterfinger.
5. Pour batter to muffin cups, about 2/3 full.
6. Bake in the oven for 20 minutes or until cupcakes are tested done. Cool in wire racks.

7. Top each cupcake with frosting and sprinkle with remaining Butterfinger.
8. Serve and enjoy.

Homemade Coconut Lime Cupcake

This delicious cupcake recipe has creamy coconut flavor that is balanced with zesty lime.

Preparation Time: 15minutes
Total Time: 45 minutes
Yield: 12servings

Ingredients

2 tablespoons lime juice
1 teaspoon lime zest, freshly grated
2/3 cup coconut milk
¼ cup coconut oil
½ teaspoon pure vanilla extract

¾ cup brown sugar
1 cup all-purpose flour, sifted
1/3 cup coconut flour, sifted
1 teaspoon baking powder
½ teaspoon baking soda
¼ teaspoon salt
Ready to use whipped vanilla frosting
Finely grated lime zest, for sprinkling

Method

1. Preheat the oven to 350 F. Line the muffin tin with paper cups.
2. In a medium bowl, with an electric mixer set to medium speed, mix together lime juice, zest, coconut milk, coconut oil, vanilla extract, and brown sugar.
3. Combine all-purpose flour, coconut flour, baking powder, baking soda, and salt in a separate medium bowl then slowly add into the wet mixture and mix until smooth. Do not over mix.
4. Pour batter into baking cups, about 2/3 full.

5. Bake in the oven for 20 to 25 minutes or until tested done. Place in wire racks to cool.
6. Top each cupcake with whipped vanilla frosting and sprinkle with grated lime zest.
7. Serve and enjoy.

Choco Peanut Butter Cupcake

This easy homemade cupcake recipe with chocolate and peanut butter is great for dessert or snack.

Preparation Time: 15minutes
Total Time: 45 minutes
Yield: 12 servings

Ingredients
½ cup softened butter
½ cup brown sugar
¼ cup peanut butter
2 large eggs

1 2/3 cups sifted all-purpose flour
1 ¼ teaspoons baking powder
½ teaspoon baking soda
2/3 cup milk

Choco Peanut Butter Frosting:
¾ cup ready to use chocolate frosting
½ cup whipped cream
3 tablespoons peanut butter

Method

1. Preheat the oven to 350 F. Line the muffin tin with paper cups.
2. In a large bowl, with an electric mixer set to medium speed, cream together the softened butter, brown sugar, and ¼ cup peanut butter until blended well and fluffy. Add eggs one at a time.
3. Gradually add in the flour, baking powder, and baking soda alternately with milk; mix until combined well.
4. Pour batter into baking cups, about 2/3 full.

5. Bake in the oven for 20 minutes or until tested done. Place in wire racks to cool.

6. ***To make the Choco Peanut Butter frosting:*** Beat the chocolate frosting, cream, and peanut butter in a mixing bowl using an electric mixer set to medium speed until smooth and fluffy. Transfer in a piping bag.

7. Pipe frosting on top of each cupcake in circular motion to make a swirl.

8. Serve and enjoy.

Mocha Cupcake with Chocolate Chips

This fantastic mocha cupcake recipe is can be enjoyed for breakfast or snack.

Preparation Time: 15 minutes
Total Time: 45 minutes
Yield: 12 servings

Ingredients

½ cup softened butter
2/3 cup brown sugar
2 large eggs
1 2/3 cups sifted all-purpose flour

2 tablespoons cocoa powder
1 ¼ teaspoons baking powder
½ teaspoon baking soda
2/3 cup freshly brewed coffee
2/3 cup chocolate chips

Method

1. Preheat the oven to 350 F. Line the muffin tin with paper cups.
2. In a large bowl, with an electric mixer set to medium speed, cream together the softened butter, brown sugar until blended well and fluffy. Add eggs one at a time.
3. Gradually add in the flour, cocoa powder, baking powder, and baking soda alternately with brewed coffee; mix until combined well. Fold in chocolate chips.
4. Pour batter into baking cups, about 2/3 full.
5. Bake in the oven for 20 minutes or until tested done. Place in wire racks to cool.
6. Serve and enjoy.

Buttermilk Cupcakes with Chocolate Chips

These light and fluffy cupcakes are perfect with coffee or tea.

Preparation Time: 15 minutes
Total Time: 45 minutes
Yield: 12 servings

Ingredients

½ cup vegetable oil
2/3 cup white sugar
1 teaspoon pure vanilla extract
2 large eggs
1 2/3 cups sifted all-purpose flour
1 ¼ teaspoons baking powder

½ teaspoon baking soda
2/3 cup buttermilk
2/3 cup chocolate chips

Method

1. Preheat the oven to 350 F. Line the muffin tin with paper cups.
2. In a large bowl, with an electric mixer set to medium speed, combine together the vegetable oil, white sugar, and vanilla until blended well. Add eggs one at a time.
3. Gradually add in the flour, baking powder, and baking soda alternately with buttermilk; mix until combined. Fold in chocolate chips.
4. Pour batter into baking cups, about 2/3 full.
5. Bake in the oven for 20 minutes or until tested done. Place in wire racks to cool.
6. Serve and enjoy.

Deep Dark Chocolate Cupcake

A cupcake recipe that yields a deep dark chocolate flavor.

Preparation Time: 15 minutes
Total Time: 45 minutes
Yield: 24 servings

Ingredients

2 cups all-purpose flour
¾ cup cocoa powder
1 ¼ cup brown sugar
1 teaspoon baking powder
1 teaspoon baking soda

1 teaspoon salt
2 large eggs
½ cup vegetable oil
1 cup water
1 teaspoon white vinegar

Method

1. Preheat the oven to 350 F. Line the muffin tins with baking cups.
2. In a large bowl, combine flour, cocoa powder, brown sugar, baking powder, baking soda, and salt.
3. Combine the eggs, oil, water and vinegar in a separate bowl.
4. Mix together the dry and wet ingredients until just blended and no more lumps.
5. Pour the batter into muffin cups, about 2/3 full.
6. Bake in the oven for 20 minutes or until tested done. Place in wire racks to cool.
7. Serve and enjoy.

Pineapple Carrot Cupcake

This cupcake recipe has a lot of fiber in it from the pineapple and carrots.

Preparation Time: 15 minutes
Total Time: 45 minutes
Yield: 36 servings

Ingredients

1 cup sugar
¾ cup vegetable oil
½ cup buttermilk
2 large eggs
2 ¼ cups whole wheat flour, sifted
1 1/3 teaspoon baking powder, sifted

1 1/3 teaspoon baking soda, sifted
1 teaspoon cinnamon, ground
½ teaspoon salt
1 cup carrots, finely grated
1 cup crushed pineapple

Method

1. Preheat the oven to 375 F. Line 3 muffin tins with paper cups.
2. Whisk together sugar, oil, and buttermilk in a large bowl. Add the eggs one at a time, until blended well.
3. Add the flour, baking powder, and baking soda; then cinnamon, and salt. Mix until just combined. Fold in the carrots and pineapple.
4. Pour batter onto muffin cups, about 2/3 full.
5. Bake in the oven for 20-25 minutes or until tested done. Place in wire racks to cool.
6. Serve and enjoy.

Spiced Banana Pumpkin Cupcakes

This moist cupcake recipe is made with bananas, pumpkin puree, and cinnamon.

Preparation Time: 15 minutes
Total Time: 45 minutes
Yield: 24 servings

Ingredients

1 cup brown sugar
½ cup vegetable oil
2 large eggs
2 cups all-purpose flour
½ teaspoon salt
1 teaspoon baking soda

3 medium ripe bananas, mashed
½ cup pumpkin puree
3/4 cup buttermilk
1 teaspoon cinnamon, ground

Method

1. Preheat the oven to 350 F. Line the muffin tins with paper cups.
2. In a bowl, whisk together sugar and oil. Add the eggs, mixing well before each addition.
3. Sift the flour, salt, and baking soda; add into the sugar mixture.
4. Stir in mashed bananas, pumpkin puree, buttermilk, and cinnamon. Mix well.
5. Pour batter into muffin cups, about 2/3 full.
6. Bake in the oven for 20 minutes or until tested done. Place in wire racks to cool.
7. Serve and enjoy!

Super Moist Banana Cupcakes

This cupcake recipe makes a perfect lunchbox or picnic item.

Preparation Time: 15 minutes
Total Time: 45 minutes
Yield: 24 servings

Ingredients

2/3 cup brown sugar
½ cup vegetable oil
2 large eggs
¾ cup sour cream
½ cup mashed ripe banana

1 teaspoon pure vanilla extract
1 ¾ cups all-purpose flour
1 ½ teaspoon baking powder
1 teaspoon baking soda
½ teaspoon salt
½ teaspoon ground cinnamon

Method

1. Preheat the oven to 375F. Line the muffin tins with paper cups.
2. Using a wire whisk, mix together 2/3 cup brown sugar, vegetable oil and eggs in a large bowl.
3. Add in sour cream, mashed bananas, and vanilla. Stir in the dry ingredients just until blended. Pour batter onto muffin cups evenly, about 2/3 full.
4. Bake in the oven for 18-20 minutes or until tested done. Place in wire racks to cool.
5. Serve and enjoy.

Cheese Cupcake with Vanilla Butter Cream Frosting

A cheesy cupcake recipe topped with simple vanilla butter cream frosting.

Preparation Time: 15 minutes
Total Time: 45 minutes
Yield: 18 servings

Ingredients
1 ¾ cups all-purpose flour, sifted
2 teaspoon baking powder
¼ teaspoon salt
½ cup unsalted butter
¼ cup white sugar
2 large eggs

½ cup condensed milk
½ cup sour cream
1 teaspoon pure vanilla extract
¾ cup Velveeta cheese, grated

Vanilla Butter Cream Frosting:
1 cup butter, softened
1 cup powdered sugar
1 teaspoon milk
1 teaspoon pure vanilla extract

Method

1. Preheat the oven to 350 F. Line the muffin tins with paper cups.
2. Combine the flour, baking powder and salt in a large bowl.
3. In a separate bowl, beat together the butter, sugar, eggs, condensed milk, sour cream, and vanilla extract.
4. Gradually add the flour mixture; mix until just combined.
5. Fold in Velveeta cheese until well blended.
6. Pour batter onto muffin cups, about 2/3 full.

7. Bake in the oven for about 20 minutes or until tested done. Cool in wire racks.

8. ***To make Butter Cream frosting:*** In a large mixing bowl, cream butter until fluffy then gradually add the sugar. Mix for 2-3 minutes on high speed. Add in milk and vanilla beat further 2-3 minutes until smooth and creamy. Transfer frosting in a piping bag.

9. Pipe frosting on top of each cupcake.

10. Serve and enjoy.

Chocolate Dream Cupcake

This chocolate cupcake recipe is a sure hit with the kids!

Preparation Time: 15 minutes
Total Time: 45 minutes
Yield: 18 servings

Ingredients
1 ¾ cups all-purpose flour
1 ½ teaspoons baking powder
½ teaspoon baking soda
2/3 cup pure cocoa powder
¾ cup brown sugar
½ cup buttermilk

½ cup water
½ cup vegetable oil
1 large egg
1 teaspoon pure vanilla extract
Powdered sugar, for dusting

Choco Butter Cream Frosting:
¾ cup butter
½ cup semi-sweet chocolate, melted
¼ cup powdered sugar
2 tablespoons heavy cream

Method

1. Preheat in the oven to 375 F. Line the muffin tins with baking cups.
2. In a large mixing bowl, combine the flour, baking powder, baking soda, cocoa powder, and brown sugar.
3. Mix together all the wet ingredients in a separate bowl.
4. Combine the dry and wet ingredients until just blended.
5. Pour batter onto muffin cups, about 2/3 full.

6. Bake in the oven for 15-20 minutes or until cupcakes are tested done. Cool in wire racks.

7. ***To make Choco Butter Cream frosting***: In a large mixing bowl, cream butter until fluffy then gradually add the melted chocolate, sugar, and heavy cream. Mix for 3-5 minutes on medium speed. Transfer frosting in a piping bag.

8. Pipe frosting on top of each cupcake. Dust with powdered sugar.

9. Serve and enjoy.

Red Velvet Cupcake with Cream Cheese Frosting

A simple and easy recipe that yields delectable red velvet cupcakes.

Preparation Time: 15 minutes
Total Time: 45 minutes
Yield: 18 servings

Ingredients

2 cups of all-purpose flour
1 cup of brown sugar
½ cup of cocoa powder
1 ¼ teaspoon of baking powder
1 teaspoon of baking soda

½ teaspoon of salt
1 cup of sour cream
2/3 cup of vegetable oil
2 large eggs
2 teaspoons of red food coloring
1 teaspoon of white vinegar
1 teaspoon of pure vanilla extract

Cream Cheese Frosting:
1 cup cream cheese
1 cup powdered sugar
1 tablespoon heavy cream
½ teaspoon pure vanilla extract

Method

1. Preheat the oven to 350 F. Line the muffin tins with paper cups.
2. Combine together the flour, brown sugar, cocoa powder, baking soda, and salt in a large bowl.
3. In another bowl, mix together the sour cream, vegetable oil, eggs, red food coloring, white vinegar, and vanilla extract using an electric mixer.
4. Gradually combine dry ingredients into the buttermilk mixture until well blended.

5. Pour batter into muffin cups, about 2/3 full.
6. Bake for 20-25 minutes or until tested done. Place in wire racks to cool.
7. ***To make the Vanilla Cream Cheese frosting:*** Beat together the cream cheese, cream in a large mixing bowl until smooth and fluffy, about 2-3 minutes. On a low speed, gradually add in the powdered sugar until combined. Add the cream and vanilla extract. Shift the speed to medium high and mix further 3 minutes. Transfer frosting in a piping bag with star tip.
8. Pipe frosting on top of each cupcake.
9. Serve and enjoy.

Les Ilagan

Orange Ginger Cupcake

A perfect blend of flavors from the orange and ginger.

Preparation Time: 15 minutes
Total Time: 50 hour
Yield: 24 servings

Ingredients
2 cups self-rising flour
½ teaspoon salt
¾ cup unsalted butter, at room
temperature
1 cup white sugar
2 eggs, at room temperature
1 teaspoon fresh ginger, grated

1 tablespoon orange zest
¾ cup whole milk, divided
¼ cup fresh orange juice

Method

1. Preheat the oven to 350 F. Line the muffin tins with paper cups.

2. Combine flour and salt in a small bowl. Set aside.

3. In a large bowl, beat butter set to high speed for 1 minute using an electric mixer. Add the sugar gradually, about ¼ cups at a time on medium speed until combined. Scrape sides of bowl, if needed. Beat for at least 2 minutes more until light and fluffy. Add in the eggs, beat well after each addition. Stir in ginger.

4. At low speed, add the flour mixture, milk, and orange juice onto the butter mixture until just combined.

5. Spoon batter to muffin cups, about 2/3 full. Smooth out batter using the back of a spoon.
6. Bake in the oven for 20 minutes or when tested done. Place in wire racks to cool.
7. Serve and enjoy.

Party Chocolate Cupcake

This chocolate cupcake topped with chocolate-butter frosting and candy sprinkles is perfect for parties.

Preparation Time: 15 minutes
Total Time: 45 minutes
Yield: 18 servings

Ingredients
1 ½ cups cake flour
¾ cup brown sugar
½ teaspoon baking soda
½ cup cocoa powder
½ teaspoon salt
1 cup water

½ cup vegetable oil

Chocolate-Butter Frosting:
¾ cup butter
¼ cup icing sugar
¾ cup dark chocolate, melted and cooled

Method

1. Preheat the oven to 375F. Line the muffin tins with paper cups.
2. In a large bowl, combine flour, sugar, baking soda, cocoa powder, and salt.
3. Stir in the water and vegetable oil. Mix until smooth.
4. Pour batter onto muffin cups, about 2/3 full.
5. Bake in the oven for 18 to 22 minutes or until tested done. Place in wire racks to cool.
6. ***To make Chocolate-Butter frosting:*** Using an electric mixer on high speed beat the butter. Gradually add the icing sugar and

continue beating for 1-2 minutes more. Slowly add the melted chocolate. Place in a piping bag then using a star tip, pipe the chocolate frosting onto the cupcakes in circular motion to make a swirl. Sprinkle with candy sprinkles.

7. Serve and enjoy!

18528227R00081

Printed in Great Britain
by Amazon